Spring

© Blake Publishing 2003
Additional material © A & C Black Publishers Ltd 2005

First published 2003 in Australia by Blake Education Pty Ltd

This edition published 2005 in the United Kingdom by
A & C Black Publishers Ltd, 37 Soho Square, London W1D 3QZ
www.acblack.com

ISBN-10: 0-7136-7267-6
ISBN-13: 978-0-7136-7267-1

A CIP record for this book is available from the British Library.

Written by Katy Pike
Design and layout by The Modern Art Production Group
Photos by John Foxx, Photodisc, Corel, Brand X, Corbis, Rubberball,
Photo Alto, Comstock and Eyewire.

UK series consultant: Julie Garnett

Printed in China by WKT Company Ltd.

A & C Black uses paper produced with elemental chlorine-free pulp,
harvested from managed sustainable forests.

Contents

Signs of Spring

As winter turns to spring, what changes can you see and feel?

Spring days are warmer. Each day is a little longer than the one before.

Plants begin to grow again. Spring **bulbs**, such as tulips and daffodils, flower.

Sheep, cows and many other animals have babies in spring.

Daffodils flower in spring.

Some birds build nests and lay eggs.

Many lambs are born in spring.

GO FACT!

DID YOU KNOW?

The spring equinox is on March 20th or 21st when day and night each last for 12 hours.

5

Plants in Spring

Warmer weather helps many plants grow in spring.

Green shoots break through the earth. Spring bulbs **sprout** and grow flowers.

The buds on trees open. The first leaves appear. Fruit trees, such as apple and cherry trees, are covered in flowers.

Cherry blossoms

Daffodils grow in large clumps.

GO FACT!

OLDEST!
A cherry tree in Japan is more than 2000 years old.

Apple trees are covered in blossom in spring.

7

Many seeds can be planted in spring.

Spring is a busy time in the garden. Gardeners plant seeds and young plants called **seedlings**.

Young plants must not dry out. They need water to live and grow. Young plants may also need to be **protected** from strong winds and from slugs and snails.

Beans sprouting

Vegetables need plenty of room to grow.

Lettuce grows fast and needs a lot of water.

Tomato seedlings are planted in spring.

Spring Food

Only a few fruits and vegetables ripen in spring.

Lettuce, peas, asparagus and rhubarb can be picked fresh and eaten in spring. People enjoy eating fresh, spring vegetables after the cold winter.

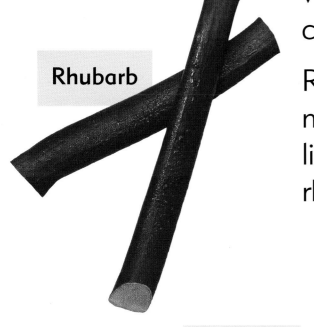

Rhubarb

Rhubarb can be used to make delicious desserts, like rhubarb crumble or rhubarb tart.

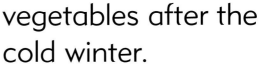

Pea pod

Asparagus

Asparagus and spring onions are being cooked.

People pick lettuce leaves in spring.

Rhubarb tastes delicious baked in a pie.

People in Spring

People spend more time outside in spring.

Spring is an exciting time outdoors. There are many new plants and animals. The air smells fresh. The cold winter is over.

The early sunrise makes waking up easier. The longer days and warm sunshine give many people more energy.

Spring clothes

Dandelions make seeds in spring.

Windy days are good for flying kites.

Early mornings are good for fishing.

Animals in Spring

Many animals have babies in spring.

Hedgehogs and dormice sleep or hibernate during the winter. In spring, they wake up and look for food. The animals are hungry after the long, cold winter.

Birds build nests and lay eggs in spring. When the chicks **hatch**, they are always hungry. The adult birds are kept busy finding food for their new chicks.

Quail eggs

Some calves are born in early spring.

This bird feeds insects to its chicks.

Rabbits have four to twelve young in a litter.

Glossary

bulb   a round root that grows into a flower or plant

hatch   when eggs break open and young birds come out

protect   to keep something safe

ripen   become ready to eat

seedling   a young plant grown from a seed

sprout   to grow new buds or shoots

Index